Condensation

William B. Rice

Consultant

Scot Oschman, Ph.D.
Palos Verdes Peninsula Unified School District
Rancho Palos Verdes, California

Publishing Credits

Dona Herweck Rice, *Editor-in-Chief*; Lee Aucoin, *Creative Director*; Don Tran, *Print Production Manager;* Timothy J. Bradley, *Illustration Manager*; Chris McIntyre, *Editorial Director*; James Anderson, *Associate Editor*; Jamey Acosta, *Associate Editor*; Jane Gould, *Editor*; Peter Balaskas, *Editorial Administrator*; Neri Garcia, *Senior Designer*; Stephanie Reid, *Photo Editor*; Rachelle Cracchiolo, M.S.Ed., *Publisher*

Image Credits

cover Olga Miltsova/Shutterstock; p.1 Olga Miltsova/Shutterstock; p.4 Marcy Maloy/Getty Images; p.5 PhotoAlto/SuperStock; p.6 Dwight Eschliman/Getty Images; p.7 Cathysbelleimage/Dreamstime; p.8 Alamy/Alaska Stock LLC; p.9 Julián Rovagnati/Shutterstock; p.10 (left) Julián Rovagnati/Shutterstock, (right) Simon Bratt/Shutterstock; p.11 ivvv1975/Shutterstock; p.12 SebStock/Shutterstock; p.13 (top) Patricia Hofmeester/Shutterstock, (bottom) Kane513/Shutterstock; p.14 Goran Cakmazovic/Shutterstock; p.15 (top) Elena Elisseeva/Shutterstock, (bottom) Sergey Lavrentev/Shutterstock; p.16 Luiz Rocha/Shutterstock; p.17 Elwynn/Shutterstock; p.18 Vesilvio/Dreamstime; p.19 Steve Cukrov/Shutterstock; p.20 Alan Egginton/Shutterstock; p.21 Michael Jung/Shutterstock; p.22 Mrorange002/Dreamstime; p.23 (top) Stephanie Reid, (bottom) Yolka/Shutterstock; p.24 Ferderic B/Shutterstock; p.25 (top) Markus Gann/Shutterstock, (bottom) Daniel Petrescu/Shutterstock; p.26 (top) Olga Miltsova/Shutterstock, (bottom) 2happy/Shutterstock; p.27 (top left) Anna Jurkovska/Shutterstock, (top right) Kristin Duvall/Getty Images, (bottom) Jorge Salcedo/Shutterstock; p.28 Rocket400 Studio/Shutterstock; p.29 Ana Clark; p.32 Martha Davis

Teacher Created Materials
5301 Oceanus Drive
Huntington Beach, CA 92649-1030
http://www.tcmpub.com

ISBN 978-1-4333-1415-5

Printed by: 51497
Printed in: China

Table of Contents

Misty Mirror 4

Condensation Is Cool 10

The Water Cycle. 22

Appendices. .28

Lab: What Is Condensation? . . .28

Glossary. .30

Index 31

A Scientist Today 32

Misty Mirror

Take a deep breath. Blow your breath onto glass or a mirror. What happens?

Mist appears on the mirror. There is a name for the mist. It is **condensation** (kon-den-SEY-shun).

hi

Condensation happens when a **gas** becomes a **liquid**. Air is a gas. Water is a liquid. Warm air from your breath touches the cold mirror. The cold turns the air into water.

Fun Fact

Breathe out on a cold day. Your breath makes a mist. That is condensation!

Condensation Is Cool

Condensation happens every day. It happens all around you. It happens each time air cools and becomes a liquid.

condensation

Condensation is the opposite of **evaporation** (i-vap-uh-REY-shun). Evaporation happens when liquid is heated and becomes a gas.

Can you see evaporation in these pictures?

You may see condensation early each day. It is the dew on grass and other plants.

Dew on spider webs makes pretty patterns in the sun.

Condensation also happens in clouds. Water evaporates from Earth. It becomes a gas. The gas rises in the air. It cools down and becomes clouds.

Clouds are condensation.

The same thing that happens in clouds happens in your home. Put some ice in a glass. You will see water form on the glass Water forms under the glass, too. That is condensation.

Fun Fact

The condensation does not leak from the glass. It comes from the air around the glass.

You can also hold your hand over a hct bowl of soup. (Not too hot!) Your hand will become wet from the steam. That is condensation, too.

Steam from soup is evaporation. When the steam becomes liquid again, then it is condensation.

The Water Cycle

Condensation is part of the **water cycle**. The water cycle is how water changes. It changes its form.

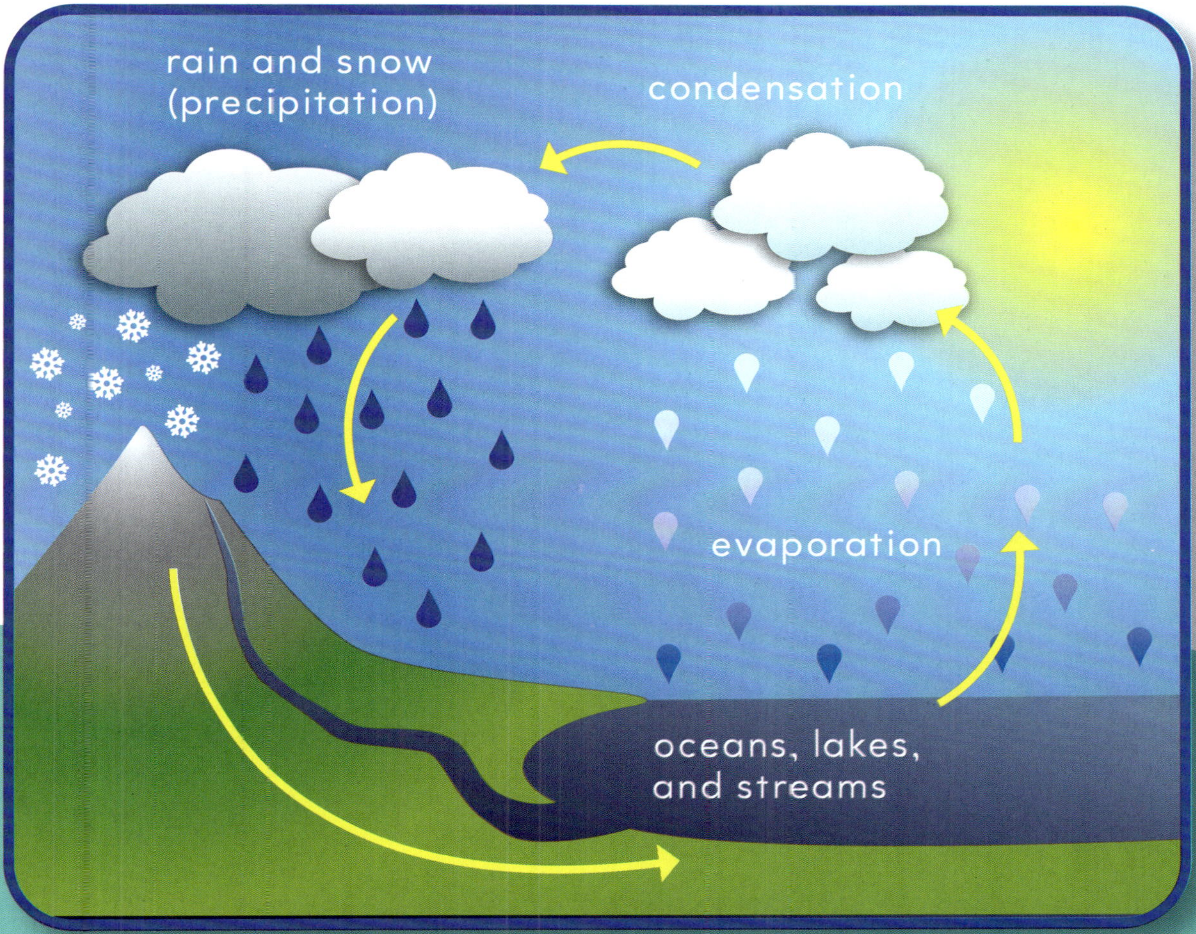
rain and snow
(precipitation)
condensation
evaporation
oceans, lakes,
and streams

Water on Earth evaporates. Then it condenses. It may fall to Earth as rain or snow. Then it evaporates again.

condensation

rain

Condensation is just one part of the water cycle. But it is a big part!

Science Lab: What Is Condensation?

See condensation in action by doing this lab.

Materials:

- 3 glasses, all the same size
- freezer
- cold colored liquid such as fruit punch

Procedure:

1. Look at the glasses. See how they are all the same.
2. Put two glasses or a table, away from each other.
3. Leave the first glass empty. Pour cold colored liquid in the second glass.
4. Put the third glass in the freezer.

5. Leave the glasses for 15 minutes.
6. Take the glass out of the freezer and put it on the table away from the others.
7. Look at the glasses. Which ones have condensation and why? The empty glass that stayed on the table has no condensation. The two other glasses have condensation. They got colder than the air around them. The warmer air touched the cold glasses. That turned the air into a liquid.

Glossary

condensation—the act of changing a gas to a liquid

evaporation—the act of changing a liquid to a gas

gas—matter that spreads out and floats in the air

liquid—matter that flows and can change shape

water cycle—the process that water goes through as it changes from one state to another.

Index

breath, 4, 8–9

clouds, 16, 18

dew, 14–15

evaporation, 12, 16, 20, 23–24

gas, 8, 12, 16

liquid, 8, 10, 12, 20

mirror, 4, 6, 8

steam, 20

water cycle, 22–26

A Scientist Today

Martha Davis is a leader. She works with other scientists to protect the most important liquid on Earth: water. Her work has helped to bring back Mono Lake in California! The lake was dying, but it is thriving again thanks to Martha and others like her.